D0471325

What Would Keanu Do?

Personal Philosophy and Awe-Inspiring Advice from the Patron Saint of Whoa

Chris Barsanti

"I'm a meathead, man. You've got smart people, and you've got dumb people. I just happen to be dumb."

THE ABOVE STATEMENT is a personal quote from the only movie star who matters right now, though you'd be forgiven for assuming it was uttered by one of his characters.

Very few actors have had to overcome the perception that their laconic presentation was a reflection of their own intellect. When Keanu appeared in the movie version of the fake talk show *Between Two Ferns*, Zach Galifianakis asked him whether it was "frustrating to have people think of you as a complete bozo, when the truth is, you're just a man with below average intelligence?" Mocking Keanu's intelligence was so widespread the Wachowskis spoofed it in *The Matrix*. After complimenting

Keanu's Neo for his cuteness, The Oracle continues with a note of catty sarcasm, "Not too bright, though."

But what has become apparent in more recent years is that in Keanu's case, still waters run deep, no matter how often he says "whoa." There is a reason filmmakers keep going back to him for roles that require soulfulness and empathy, as well as the intense focus of a surfer-warrior-monk. What initially read as vacuousness now comes across as patience, forbearance, even thoughtfulness. His real-life decency is as legendary as it is perplexing. What movie star—nay, what human being—behaves like this, particularly when no one else is looking? Even his name is a mood (Keanu means "the cool breeze under the mountains").

Keanu became a meme factory in part because his stillness and temperment draw people in. Likewise, his characters are marked not just by their abilities but by an inherent wisdom. Yes, even Johnny Utah. Even Shane Falco. Even the duller half of the Wyld Stallyns. He is a font of actionable advice, even when his example is occasionally one of inaction.

The phrase "nosce te ipsum" (know thyself) was carved into the Temple of Apollo at Delphi, making it a known maxim during the dawn of philosophy heralded by Socrates (yes, *that* Sew-crates). In this task Keanu appears to be a savant: "I'm a meathead, man." Yes, there are smart people and there are dumb people. But we'd all count ourselves closer to the former if we spent more time exploring the prescience, patience and power of the dumb people's presupposed posterboy. This book does exactly that, examining practical advice and life lessons from the one and only Keanu Reeves. But it's important to note from the outset that, much like "The One" in *The Matrix* trilogy, Keanu is a singular entity. And he wants you to be yourself.

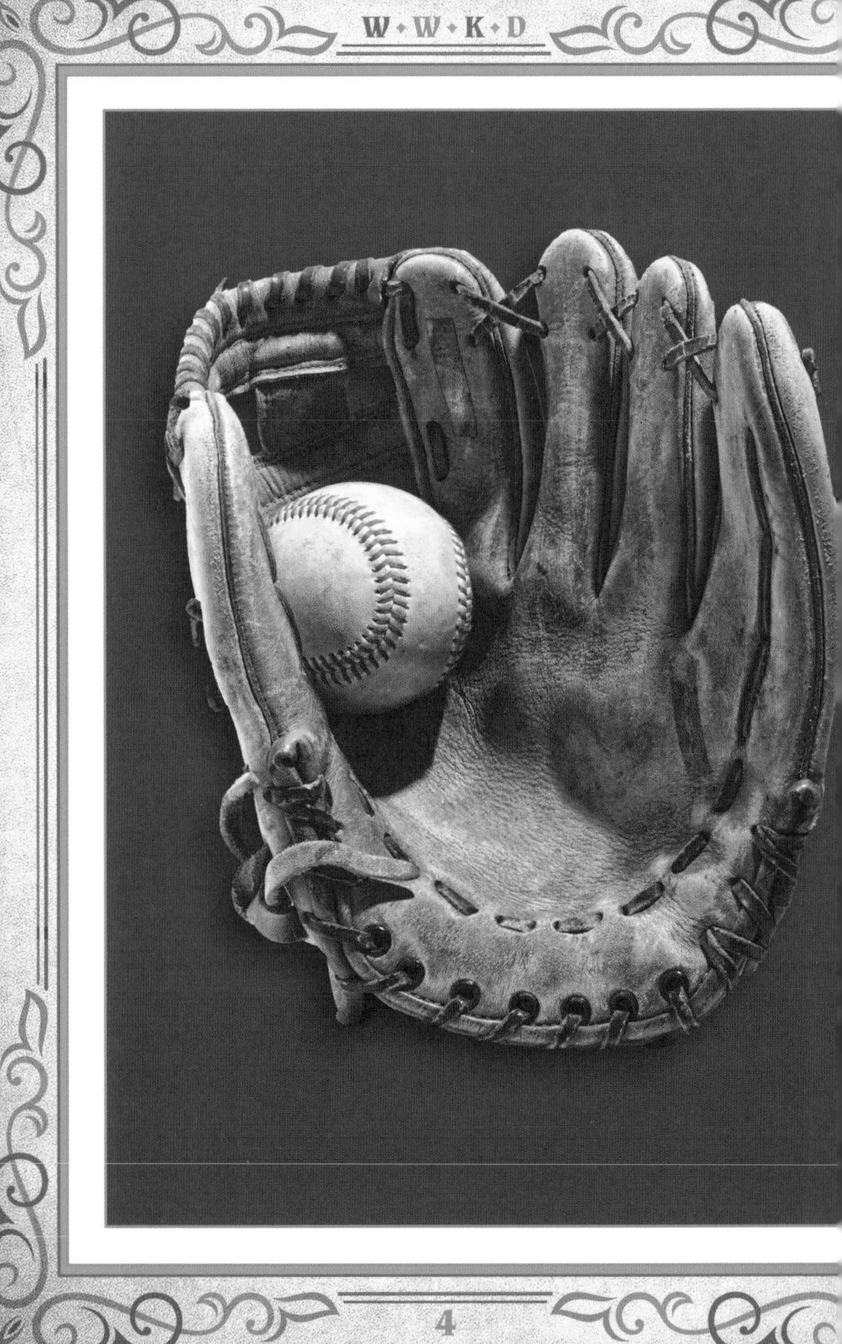

“

One of the most important things in life is showing up.

”

—Conor O’Neill, *Hardball* (2001)

Embrace Stupidity

Know that knowing nothing still means you know something. Just ask Bill & Ted.

CCORDING TO *Bill & Ted's Excellent Adventure* (1989), everything will be nothing short of righteous in the future. That's because the world was wise enough to heed the words of two burnout Bodhisattvas from San Dimas, California. Their Kant-ian delineation of the sole categorical imperative ("Be excellent to each other") proved to be a simple and rational way of crafting a fully functioning and moral society, while their Aristotelean emphasis on happiness as a supreme good ("Party on, dudes!") ensured a contented populace.

What is contentment, though? At the start of the movie, Ted "Theodore" Logan (Keanu) is far from it. He sucks at guitar, is in danger of "flunking most

Alex Winter and Keanu learn history from those who lived it.

heinously," and his dad's about to ship him off to a military boarding school. Not particularly righteous. But that's when George Carlin's Rufus appears and gives Ted and his buddy Bill S. Preston (Alex Winter) access to a handy time-traveling telephone booth in order to study up for history class.

Throughout this movie, Bill and Ted's collective intellect—or lack thereof—is fairly clear. Their general mental state is sublimely blissed-out eternal California sunshine located somewhere between *Fast Times at Ridgemont High*, hair-metal videos and the nearest mall food court. They are sober Spicolis. Pre-Lebowskis. Valley dudes. And while neither are killing it intellectually, Ted seems even less on-point than Bill. Which makes their comprehension of the different epochs they zoom through somewhat fuzzy ("Bill, those are historical babes").

"All we are is dust in the wind, dude."

Nevertheless, for all his seeming vacancy and haplessness, Ted understands a few things that may not have been apparent to most people. One is that Genghis Khan can be enticed to follow you through time with Twinkies. More crucially, Ted knows wisdom when he hears it. Bumbling through ancient Greece, he impresses Socrates with epistemological truths by way of Kansas ("All we are is dust in the wind, dude"). Then, discovering that "Sew-crates" once said, "The only true wisdom consists in knowing that you know nothing," Ted has his mind blown. "That's us, dude!"

In his ever-positive yet still self-effacing way, Ted has taken a far shorter road to wisdom than the great philosopher of antiquity. At very few points in their adventure does Ted make a point of exhibiting his knowledge. Despite having a knack for the pertinent observation ("I do not believe we will get Eddie Van Halen until we have a triumphant video"; "Strange things are afoot at the Circle K"), Ted is fully aware that he and Bill are not the brightest bulbs in San Dimas, much less the world.

For his part, after learning that the Oracle at Delphi had proclaimed "no man is wiser than Socrates," Socrates set about trying to show that the Oracle was wrong. Finding that everyone he approached tried to claim knowledge they didn't have, Socrates concluded he must be the wisest around, as nobody else appeared fully in touch with and honest about their ignorance.

Knowing just how little he knows, Ted not only exhibits humility, he shows wisdom in acknowledging—and embracing—the weakness of his ignorance. And therein lies his strength. To his own self he is true. You can do the same—accept the fact that there's more to this world than you can possibly comprehend. There's bound to be something you don't know, and that's OK. Civilizations have been built on worse foundations.

he only way to truly know a man is to play tackle football with him on a beach in the moonlight.

—*The Book of* Point Break,
Chapter 3, Verse 18

Minor Miracles from the Patron Saint of Whoa

Favorites Are Overrated

Just like Buddhist teachings have always said, all beings are created equally in the eyes of the universe (and in the eyes of Keanu).

SOME DECISIONS are just impossible, and no matter how much we'd love to be able to give a definitive answer, doing so would—at some elemental level—involve lying to ourselves. When celebrities are asked interview questions that pose such decisions, the stakes are heightened: they're not just lying to themselves, they're lying to an adoring public. Keanu often avoids such limited declarations, instead choosing to offer momentary reflections on his favorite film or co-star or food with a simple, "Today I'll say...."

Which is why, no matter how much the world might have wanted to hear Keanu's favorite animal was a sloth, or a golden retriever, or a Galapagos penguin, he knew he had to be true to himself and the entire animal kingdom. When asked his favorite animal during a Reddit AMA, he opted to give the truest answer possible: He doesn't have a favorite animal. Which leads us to the inescapable conclusion that he loves all animals equally, and would go full-blown John Wick on anyone who tried to harm one. Take it from Keanu: Make the effort to treat every living being with respect and love. Except maybe dog murderers.

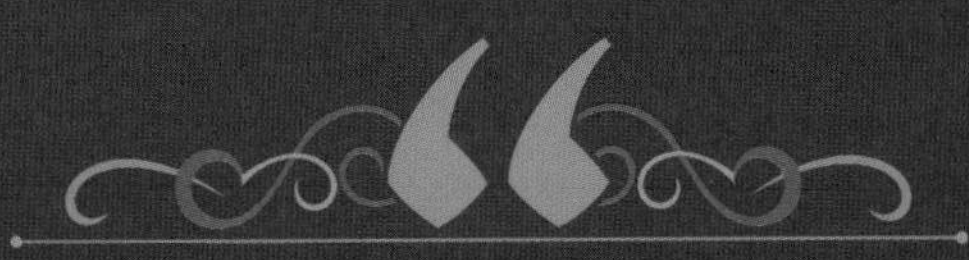

The simple act of paying attention can take you a long way.

”

—Keanu Reeves

State Your Value

I Love You to Death *illustrates that just because you've been underestimated doesn't mean you don't have worth.*

N *I LOVE YOU TO DEATH* (1990)—a droll, criminally underrated comedic take on a sensational tabloid story about a cheating husband who survives, Rasputin-like, an onslaught of murder attempts—Keanu is absent for most of the story. At first glance, you might think his Marlon character is just there for comic relief. Marlon first appears in an opiate fog, levering himself up from underneath a pool table with eyes as vacant as saucers and hair that looks like it has been attacked by a sentient pair of clippers with something to prove. But to some degree, this is all a ruse. Marlon is in actuality yet another Keanu character whose seeming vacancy obscures reservoirs of deeper thought.

William Hurt and Keanu in *I Love You to Death*.

Marlon and his cousin Harlan (William Hurt) are being propositioned by Devo (River Phoenix) to help kill Joey (Kevin Kline), the philandering pizza-man husband to Devo's not-so-secret crush Rosalie (Tracey Ullman). You might expect an apparent dirtbag like Marlon to instantly jump at the offer. But even behind the mental hum of misfiring synapses, he's cannier than that. Even semi-comatose, Marlon understands he has some worth. He knows Devo would not be asking him to help with this task if he could do it himself. Since, in 1990, you couldn't just go to TaskRabbit and punch in "Contract Killer (discreet, inexpensive)," Marlon also knows that Devo has a limited pool of people he can go to for something like this. Rather than leaping at the first offer, he bargains for more money: "If we're going to waste the dude, we oughta get paid for it, man." It's stoner logic, but the stoner has a point.

"If we're going to waste the dude, we oughta get paid for it, man."

Marlon then ups the ante by pushing his point home with, "I mean, that's the American way, right?" He is being asked to provide a service, after all, and in many ways has the market cornered. Why should he be expected to provide this service for free? Marlon also makes clear he is no worse than the person who is offering him the money. Later, the moral confusion that Marlon is preemptively pushing back on here comes up when Rosalie says to Devo in hypocritically moralizing horror, "You hired drug addicts?" to which her mother Nadja (Joan Plowright) says soothingly, "Don't think of them as drug addicts. Think of them as killers."

But Marlon is no more just a drug addict than he is just a killer: he's an independent contractor with at least a handful of skills. As Brad Pitt's assassin says in *Killing Them Softly*, "In America, you're on your own. America's not a country, it's just a business." Marlon is a true-blue American. Sure, he's a little shaky reciting the Pledge of Allegiance ("deliver us from freedom"). But what could be more American than the moment when Marlon is distracted with childhood glee after realizing the baseball bat with which he is about to bust open Joey's head is a Reggie Jackson limited edition? This shows Marlon to be just the latest in a long line of American entrepreneurs with an individualistic streak and a comfortable attitude toward the deployment of violence. As Nadja reassures Rosalie, "In America, people kill each other left and right. Is like national pastime."

Marlon also represents a transitional stage for the evolution of Keanu, the end of the beginning, one might say. Coming out a year after *Bill & Ted's Excellent Adventure* and just one year before *Point Break*, *I Love You to Death* shows Keanu's character grappling with the boundaries of his own agency. As part of that struggle, he understands that the first step forward is to define his own worth. Otherwise, the world will define it for him. This was true for Keanu. The same holds true for you.

CHICAGO

If you discover a world-changing secret, maybe keep it to yourself.

—*The Book of* Chain Reaction,
Chapter 7, Verse 9

Minor Miracles from the Patron Saint of Whoa

Being Sad Doesn't Mean You're Defeated

His life has been unhinged by tragedy, but Keanu has never let that darkness define his life.

IT'S EASY TO WALLOW in defeat or self-pity or sadness when we're feeling down, and the temptation to let ourselves be swallowed by despair can be overwhelming. This is doubly true after tragedies like losing a best friend, girlfriend and baby in the same decade, which is part of the reason why the mythos of "Sad Keanu" has gained such traction in the world of the meme. Many celebrities would be less than thrilled at an image of themselves eating alone on a park bench becoming an iconic one. But when a BBC interviewer brought up the fact that he seems to give off the aura of carrying tremendous burdens of grief, Keanu laughed off the suggestion. Sure, he's been through plenty, but so have millions of us. It does no good to focus on the negative events in our lives over which we had little or no control; instead, Keanu chooses to proactively channel his grief into good deeds, whether that means helping folks stranded on the side of the road, endowing a children's hospital or simply carrying himself with the impenetrable aura of a down-to-earth dude. Paying it forward feels a lot better than letting life grind you down. Next time you're sad, be happy you can still enjoy a sandwich in the sun.

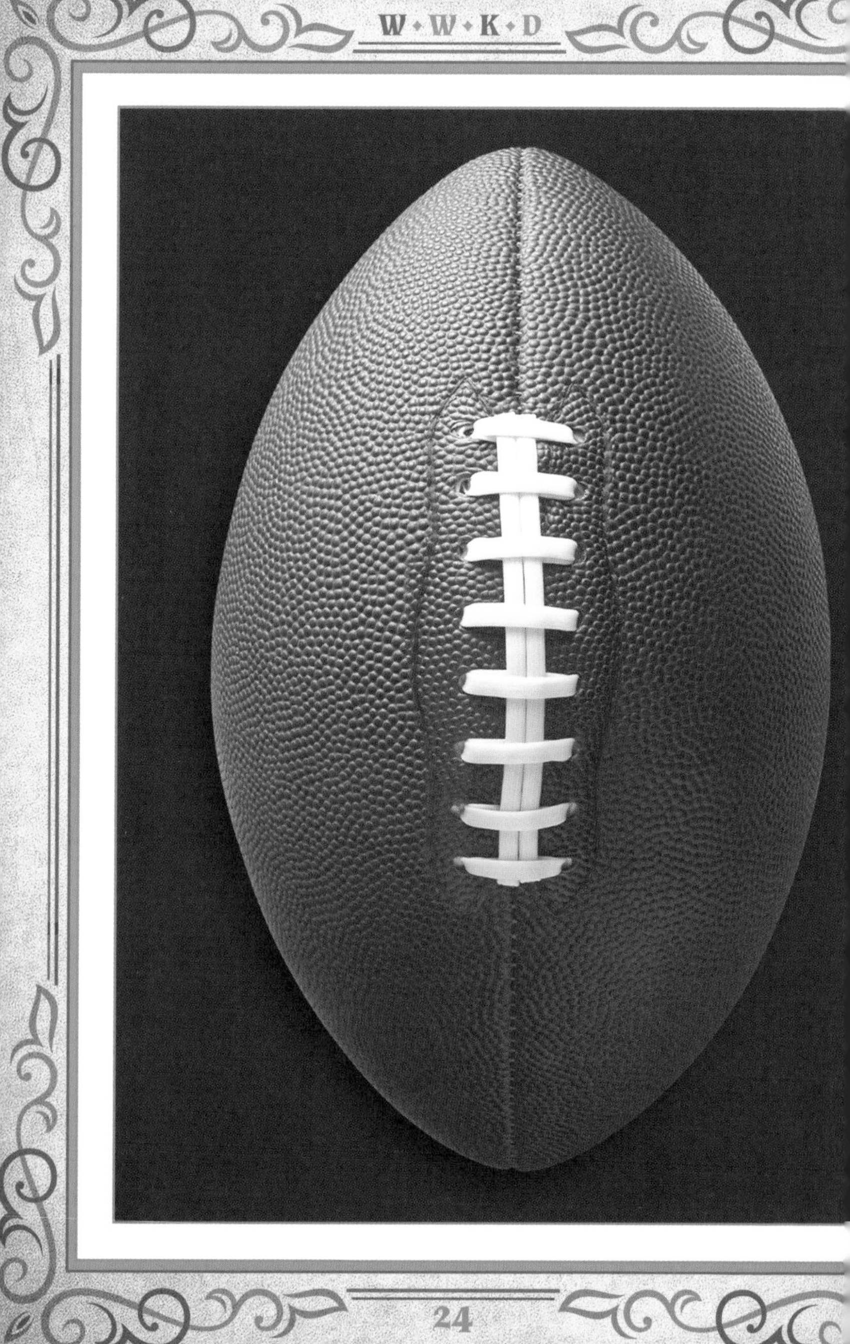

Pain heals. Chicks dig scars. Glory lasts forever.

—Shane Falco,
The Replacements (2000)

Keep Moving Forward

A key takeaway from *My Own Private Idaho* is to keep your eyes either ahead or down. Never explain. Never complain. Do not look back.

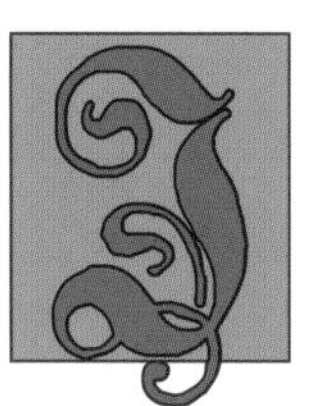

IN GUS VAN SANT'S *My Own Private Idaho* (1991), Keanu is something of a shapeshifter. Much of the movie is set among the homeless hustlers on the rain-spattered streets of Portland, Oregon. One hustler, Keanu's Scott Favor, seems more put together than the others. He's first spotted by Mike (River Phoenix) in a mansion whose owner they have been hired to pleasure. Like many of the hustlers, Mike is rangy and scattered, always looking over his shoulder. But even though Scott sleeps on a building rooftop just like Mike, he appears right at home in that wood-paneled library.

River Phoenix and Keanu gear up for a journey.

This makes sense, as Scott is a prince of the city. On his fast-approaching 21st birthday, he is set to inherit a Scrooge McDuck-like pile of money from his father, the mayor. Like Shakespeare's Prince Hal, upon whom Van Sant drew liberally for the script, Scott slums by choice. Unlike Mike—desperately in love with Scott, who claims not to be gay and to only have sex with men for money—he sees living on the street as more game than necessity. Scott spells out his plan in an alleyway soliloquy, saying "When I am 21, I won't want

"When I left home, the maid asked me where I was off to. I said, 'Wherever. Whatever. Have a nice day.'"

any more of this life" and muses about how his parents would be more impressed by his dramatic change "than if I'd been a good son all along." This statement rhymes less prettily than Hal's version ("I'll so offend, to make offence a skill; Redeeming time when men think least I will") but nevertheless gets the point across.

At this point, Keanu's well-meaning dunce persona had been barely tweaked by that same year's *Point*

Break, which added marksmanship and extreme-sports cred to his standard character skillset. But Scott's casual, lived-in, ripcord confidence and sly intelligence were new for Keanu. They give his Scott an optimism and buoyancy that his more down-and-out companions can't or won't access.

Scott is destined to leave the streets behind and ignore his old friends once his money rolls in, and there's certainly a cold selfishness to that arc. But it's leavened by a thoughtful appreciation of the freedom his background provides. After Mike collapses in one of his narcoleptic fits, Scott tenderly arranges him in an out-of-the-way spot and gives him a kind of good-night benediction, "When you wake up, wipe the slugs off your face. Be ready for a new day." It's a small thing, but a rare note of kindness in a story marked more by thievery and scams.

Later, Mike and Scott are resting by a campfire and talking about their pasts. Scott says, "When I left home, the maid asked me where I was off to. I said, 'Wherever. Whatever. Have a nice day.'" While it's easier to embrace a bohemian lifestyle when there's a trust fund to fall back on, your past is less important when all that matters is your future. No matter how many slugs have slinked their way over you, always remember you possess the power to slap them out of your hair and begin anew.

To excel at board games is to master Death itself.

—*The Book of* Bill & Ted's Bogus Journey, *Chapter 2, Verse 31*

KEANECDOTES

Minor Miracles from the Patron Saint of Whoa

Roll With the Punches

When few would have, Keanu went out of his way to make some unlucky fellow travelers feel like it was their best day ever.

ANYONE CAN BE FORGIVEN for not being at their best on a day when their plane is forced to make an emergency landing before it's reached its destination. But when Keanu's flight from San Francisco to Burbank was grounded at Bakersfield following mechanical issues, he proved himself unfazed by either the danger of the plane's problems or the inconvenience of landing somewhere he didn't need to be.

In fact, he kept spirits up on the incredibly intimate Bakersfield-to-Burbank van chartered by the airline, sharing trivia about Bakersfield, playing song clips of "Bakersfield Sound" country music for his fellow passengers, revealing details of his pit stop fuel up (a Gatorade and a banana) and just acting like a regular dude. The lesson: If you stay true to yourself, you can make the best of a bad situation, and help others in the process.

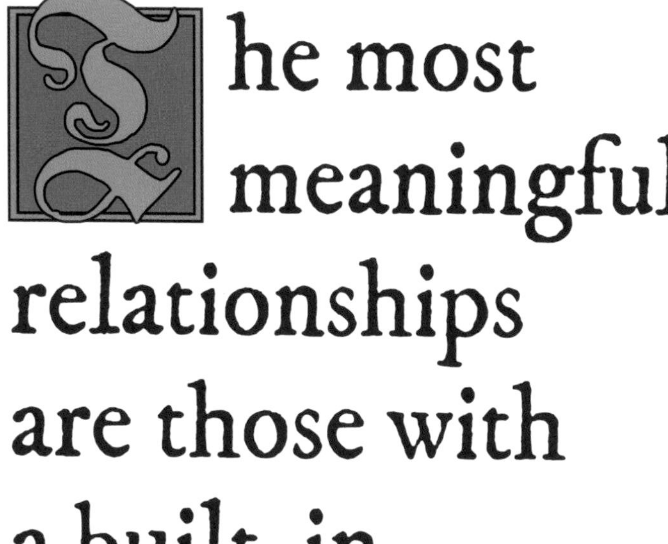

The most meaningful relationships are those with a built-in expiration date.

—*The Book of* Sweet November,
Chapter 11, Verse 30

ARCH

Minor Miracles from the Patron Saint of Whoa

Serve Others, Regardless of Status

Every human story is valuable and worthwhile—it's easy to forget, but Keanu can help us remember.

WHEN KEANU WAS OUT on the town with friends at Manhattan's Lucky Strike Lanes in 2016, he could have been forgiven for focusing on keeping his hooks out of the gutter and his pals entertained. But as should be clear by this point, such is not the Keanu way. While stepping outside to field a phone call, Keanu noticed a homeless man asking passersby for spare change. He readily opened his wallet for the man, but didn't stop where most of us would have. After striking up a conversation, Keanu asked the man if he'd like a bite to eat, going back into Lucky Strike to get a hot meal. He then brought it back out and sat with the man while he ate. Keanu fans immediately noted the incident's similarity to a 1997 happening, when Keanu was photographed sitting and chatting with a vagrant in LA for an entire afternoon, proof that where others might see a homeless man, Keanu sees a man, with or without a home. No matter what day of the week, kindness can be just as meaningful as cash. Share both when you can.

“It’s fun to be hopelessly in love. It’s dangerous, but it’s fun.”

—Keanu Reeves

Be Gracious in Victory

Dangerous Liaisons suggests chivalry isn't dead—it's just underrated.

IN THE 1782 epistolary novel of French aristocratic decadence, *Dangerous Liaisons*, the honorable and fairly dim Chevalier Danceny, finding his honor besmirched, challenges the dishonorable and highly intelligent Vicomte de Valmont to a duel, writing of "the odious abuse you made of my blind confidence." In Stephen Frears's whipsmart, acidly funny and unexpectedly tragic adaptation some two centuries later, Keanu plays Danceny with the kind of slow-witted but big-hearted radiant decency that made up a good part of his resume (and, let's face it, public persona) at the time. Caught up in the gladiatorial romantic warfare waged by Valmont (John Malkovich) and his co-conspirator the Marquise de Merteuil (Glenn Close), Danceny is like Bambi being stalked by two hunters. What's worse—he thinks of them as Thumper and

Keanu and John Malcovich's Valmont have a gentlemen's disagreement.

Flower. Nevertheless, he is nearly the only character to emerge from this tale with even a shred of dignity.

Danceny pops up occasionally as a well-meaning sop. First spotted crying at the opera, he is introduced to a smitten Cécile de Volanges (Uma Thurman) by Merteuil, who describes him as "one of those rare eccentrics who come here to listen to the music." Later, irritated by Danceny's painfully slow seduction of de Volanges mucking up her plans, Merteuil notes that "like most intellectuals, he's intensely stupid." Given the doe-eyed credulousness with which Danceny treats all of Merteuil and Valmont's scheming, her diagnosis seems not far off the mark.

But while the backbone of the movie is the tart back-and-forth between Merteuil and Valmont—which shades from playfully decadent to chillingly soulless—its last act is centered on Keanu's Danceny. After spending much of the story as an off-screen punchline, once he challenges Valmont to a duel, the

"He had good cause. I don't believe that's something anyone has ever been able to say about me."

clumsy Danceny barely hangs on to his sword, a far cry from the dextrous blademasters Keanu plays in later movies like *47 Ronin*. But Valmont, wrenched with guilt and sickened of life after being goaded by Merteuil's jealousy into abandoning the only woman he ever truly loved, Madame de Tourvel (Michelle Pfeiffer), he falls on Danceny's sword.

What follows is a character-revealing moment. As Valmont bleeds out on the snow, Danceny sits at his side and listens to his foe's dying words. Danceny is skeptical of Valmont's warning about Merteuil ("in this affair we are both her creatures"), saying "You must permit me to treat with skepticism anything you have to say about her." Being desperately in love with de Volange hasn't kept Danceny from letting Merteuil use him as her boy toy. But Danceny agrees nevertheless to take a dying declaration of love from his sworn enemy to Tourvel (who is also dying, in her case from a broken heart—love is a literal battlefield here).

"He had good cause," Valmont says somewhat laconically about Danceny's killing him. "I don't believe that's something anyone has ever been able to say about me." In a story packed with lies and pettiness and vengeance, Danceny is nearly the only member of the nobility who wouldn't make the local peasantry want to sharpen their pitchforks. In victory, rather than Merteuil's "win or die" philosophy of life or Valmont's vapid trickster cruelty, Danceny shows grace and humility, bowing his head in agony at the life he has just taken. In this way, Danceny follows the usually ignored 11th century chivalric code ("Chevalier" meaning "knight"), which demanded generosity in victory. Danceny's excellently valorous behavior toward his tormentor shows that intelligence and wit do not always equate to virtue.

So be kind. Sure, the stuff-shirted cynics might view you as a sap—but at least you'll be able to live with yourself.

The odds of Buddha being reincarnated as a Caucasian boy are one in three.

—*The Book of* Little Buddha, *Chapter 2, Verse 18*

IN THEATERS AND
TMAS DA
ATERS AND real 3D

KEANECDOTES

Minor Miracles from the Patron Saint of Whoa

Keep Yourself in Check

The words "celebrity" and "respectful" don't usually come up in random word associations, but for Keanu they're more than compatible.

THE 21ST CENTURY is lousy with tales of celebrities using their station to get whatever they want, whenever they want, regardless of legality or morality. The #MeToo movement has blown a crater in the entertainment industry, and sifting through the rubble has revealed more horror stories than uplifting tales. One celebrity, however, stands out in the mindfulness he displays at every turn, maintaining respect for everyone he encounters, no matter the circumstances. Keanu, it turns out, is unsurprisingly an A-lister who can teach the rich and powerful everywhere a lesson. Perhaps the most illustrative example of Keanu as living proof that gentlemanly respect is alive and well is the way he takes photos with fans. Realizing that just because someone is a fan and asks for a picture doesn't mean they want to be pawed by their idol, Keanu mimics a friendly arm-around-the-shoulder or -waist pose without actually touching, offering a wholesome memento without any awkwardness. The lesson: Respect is earned, particularly when it's deserved. And it's always a two-way street.

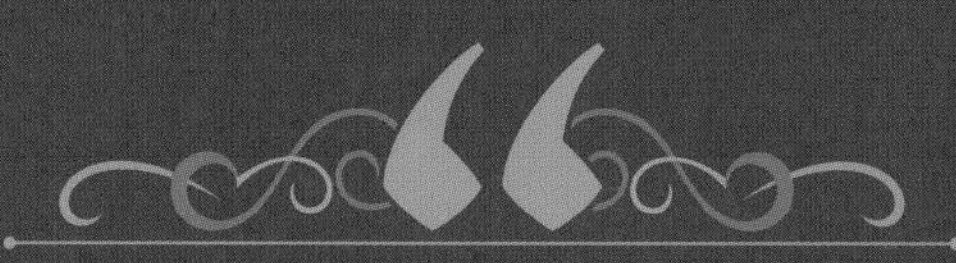

You must resign yourself to being extraordinary.

—Harry,
The Last Time I Committed Suicide (1997)

Trust Your Gut

For Point Break's Johnny Utah, *buying two meatball subs is a lesson in listening to your instincts.*

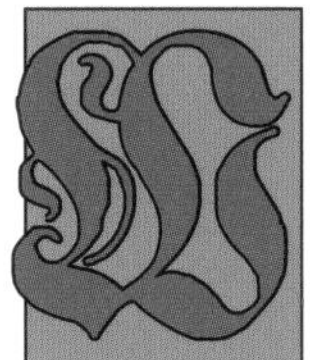

HEN YOU'RE ON a stakeout trying to investigate a group of bank robbers looting Los Angeles, it's imperative to be at your best. A brilliant realization or break in the case—such as the fact that the criminals you're pursuing are actually surfers, whose heists coincide with areas where the swells are the most righteous—won't come to a distracted mind. This is a lesson Keanu's Johnny Utah learns from his more experienced partner, Angelo Pappas, early on in *Point Break* (1991), but it's reiterated later, as the duo waits outside a bank they believe to be vulnerable. Pappas apparently determines his performance is not up to his usual standards (whatever they may be) due to a decided lack of

Keanu and Gary Busey gear up to catch waves and bad guys.

mental satisfaction. The only remedy? Italian-American cuisine.

"Right around that corner, there is a sandwich shop," Pappas—memorably played by Gary Busey—instructs Johnny Utah. "They sell meatball sandwiches, best I ever tasted. Would you go get me two?" The eccentric detective knows exactly what he needs to get back on track, and trusts his gut that it's the right time to act. Pappas is so certain, he literally doubles down: "Utah! Get me two!"

"They sell meatball sandwiches. Best I ever tasted. Would you go get me two?"

Sure enough, as Johnny Utah is picking up two meatball sandwiches, a tuna on wheat and two lemonades, a suspicious looking car pulls up outside the bank. Getting back into the car with the sandwiches, Utah asks if Pappas has noticed the car. From here, the *Point Break* script picks up the action perfectly: "Pappas is about to take a huge bite when a meatball falls out of the end of the sandwich. It lands on the seat next to him. He looks at it. Picks it up. Pops it into his mouth and—Freezes, mouth open.

Eyes focused on...The Ex-Presidents, in living color, flashing through the doors of the bank 80 feet away."

We usually think of the cliché "trust your gut" as having more to do with sticking to your first impressions, but one of the many things Keanu's films can teach us is that sometimes the truth behind it is more simple. Pappas subconsciously knew something was up, like a wild animal sensing a storm. His body interprets that instinct through a need for comfort and security: hunger pangs. He might not have realized what was going on, but by the time Johnny Utah saw that car pull up, he understood that his partner had had the most accurate "gut feeling" of his investigative career.

Utah carries this lesson forward through the rest of the film, eventually discovering the Ex-Presidents are led by his surf guru bestie Bodhi (who, unfortunately for Utah, follows his gut as well, and had put a plan in motion to blackmail Utah into joining the Ex-Presidents for good). After Bodhi (Patrick Swayze) escapes, Utah's gut knows exactly where to find him—ready to take on the life-threatening surf off Australia's Bells Beach during a "50-year storm." Naturally, he gets his man.

Next time you feel a rumble in your stomach, understand that it might not simply be a hankering for grub—you could be in the midst of a game-changing event. Act accordingly.

Even in the most heated of arguments with your in-laws, arson is never the answer.

—*The Book of* A Walk in the Clouds,
Chapter 21, Verse 4

TNT

KEANECDOTES

Minor Miracles from the Patron Saint of Whoa

You Only Have One Mother. Act Accordingly.

It takes a special kind of in-demand Hollywood bachelor to take his mom to the biggest party of the year.

THE OSCARS is the culmination of a months-long awards season that sees the best actors and filmmakers of the year let loose after campaigning week after week for their latest work. The afterparties are legendary, and the ceremony itself has, in recent years, shrugged off many of its more serious trappings in favor of a more jovial atmosphere. In short, it's the night when Hollywood's most beautiful and talented people get together and party their expertly made-up faces off. So when Keanu, enjoying a career renaissance thanks to films like *John Wick*, showed up to the 2020 ceremony with his mother, the world took notice. On a night when he could have asked anyone in Los Angeles to accompany him to the biggest party of the year without fear of rejection, Keanu chose to share the once-in-a-lifetime event with the most important woman in his life. Always remember where you came from—fame is fickle, but family is family.

“They’ll negotiate; they’re corporate.”

—Johnny Mnemonic,
Johnny Mnemonic (1995)

Keep Calm and Carry On

Bram Stoker's Dracula and the value of always being polite. Even with the undead.

RANCIS FORD COPPOLA'S maximalist take on the vampire movie, *Bram Stoker's Dracula* (1992), went for the jugular, so to speak. No more with the stoic, lurking vampires of an earlier cinematic era, wafting about in capes and evening attire. Instead, Coppola got back to Stoker's portrayal of Dracula: an essentially foreign villain from a strange and remote Eastern land who is contrasted with the wholesome decency of his British hero. Which is why when Keanu's Jonathan Harker—a humble young solicitor who doesn't seem to have ever set foot outside the British Isles, or wanted to—encounters the lugubriously threatening Count Dracula (Gary Oldman) in his Transylvania castle, he doesn't just say, "Good day, sir!" and storm out. It wouldn't be polite.

Keanu and Gary Oldman trade hair care secrets.

Yes, even in dealing with a centuries-old mad man who could fly, turn himself into rats and would later try to make Harker's fiancée his own undead bride, Keanu's character seems motivated by that most classic of Britishisms: "Keep calm and carry on." Most people would have turned right around the moment they were lifted off the ground by a claw-handed creature and deposited into a carriage surrounded by howling wolves, but Harker is a different breed. Having thought he was in Transylvania on legitimate business, he carries on as though everything were above board and normal. As though his host didn't wrap himself in brocaded gowns, have skin that looks like lumps of uncooked dough and continually make ominous jokes to himself ("I never drink ... wine").

When Harker makes a comment that offends Dracula, the vampire objectively overreacts, grabbing a broadsword and swinging it at Harker with a snarl. Once again, the average human might have responded with fury, run off into the night or just fainted in terror. But Harker, the soul of decorum, remains quiet at first, and then says the most astonishing thing: "I have offended you with my ignorance, Count. Forgive me."

Having little recourse for escape, all Harker can do is fall back on his own superpower: well-practiced etiquette.

A common trope in horror movies is the blithe dolt, who blunders ahead despite danger staring him in the face. Harker's passivity after having a sword jammed at him could be interpreted as slow-wittedness of the Ted "Theodore" Logan variety ("Vlad is totally going to impale us, dude"). But this isn't ignorance. This is its close cousin: upper crust civility. Harker already senses he is trapped in a remote place with a curious creature who seems a bit too enamored of blood and a little too unnerved by crucifixes. Having little recourse for escape, all Harker can do is fall back on his own superpower: well-practiced etiquette. The objective of Victorian-era politeness according to *The Gentleman's Book of Etiquette* (1860) is "to put all at their ease." And it's a good thing he does. Yes, in the end, Harker is nearly killed by Dracula, set upon by a harem of undead brides, and forced to confront the Count blade in hand after the villain absconds with his betrothed. But that's hardly an escalation—it's an entirely appropriate response. And in this, Harker is still acting in a way that won't sully his reputation.

The lesson here is that in all things you must carry yourself with equal doses of confidence and humility. As the aforementioned *Gentleman's Book of Etiquette* suggests: "The principal rules of politeness are, to subdue the temper, to submit to the weakness of our fellow men, and to render to all their due, freely and courteously. These, with the judgment to recommend ourselves to those whom we meet in society, and the discrimination to know when and to whom to yield, as well as the discretion to treat all with the deference due to their reputation, station, or merit, comprise, in general, the character of a polite man, over which the admission of even one blot or shade will throw a blemish not easily removed."

Or rather, better to keep your cool and act a gentleman than to live rashly as a blood-sucking pestilence on society.

Some threats are so existential they require more than 46 disgraced samurai.

—*The Book of* 47 Ronin,
Chapter 9, Verse 12

Minor Miracles from the Patron Saint of Whoa

Live For Your Ride-or-Dies

The famously motorbike-mad Keanu chose a unique way of expressing his gratitude to his tireless stunt team.

ONE OF THE MOST defining action sequences of *The Matrix* trilogy comes in *The Matrix Reloaded* when Neo is set against 100 copies of Agent Smith in an epic battle. But off-camera, pulling off the scene involved Keanu and a dozen stuntmen executing the same brutal slams and hits for weeks on end. For Keanu, ice baths became a regular necessity as he and the stuntmen delved deeper and deeper into the five-and-a-half minute fight sequence. Keanu was so impressed by the stunt team's willingness to continue with such a taxing regimen for the sake of a great scene that he took it upon himself to personally thank them for their dedication. After all, this single scene involved more martial arts moves than the entirety of the first *Matrix* film. So after filming wrapped, each of the 12 stunt performers came to set to find a handpicked gift from Keanu: a brand new Harley-Davidson motorcycle. The lesson: Give credit where it's due to keep everybody moving forward—no gas required.

“There is no spoon.”

—Neo, *The Matrix* (1999)

Embrace the Random

Constantine *posits that there is no existential plan and that to thrive in chaos, you must accept all its implications.*

HE WORLD OF the angels-and-demons supernatural thriller *Constantine* (2005) is supposed to have rules. But not everybody plays by them. That's the conundrum faced by Keanu's John Constantine, the longtime comic-book antihero who operates as a kind of roving exorcist, a downbeat knight errant who tries to keep pure evil from breaking into the human world through demonic possessions. In this Machiavellian rendering of *Paradise Lost*, God and the Devil are playing a strategic game: devils and angels can't do anything directly on the human plane but they can influence good or bad behavior, scoring points for their side. "They call it the balance," Constantine

Keanu and Rachel Weisz get ready to go through hell.

grumps between innumerable cigarettes, "I call it hypocritical bullshit."

Constantine's problem with this so-called balance is the pointlessness of adhering to rules that are made essentially meaningless by their being constantly flouted. He tries to explain this to Angela (Rachel Weisz), an overwhelmed police detective getting a crash course in the Eternal Battle Between Good and

Evil. She tries, as any person would once seeing what lies behind the veil of reality, to figure out the rhyme and reason of her new reality. Constantine quickly disabuses her of that idea: “God’s a kid with an ant farm, lady. He’s not planning anything.”

This sentiment should be anathema to a world that presents as regulated to the nth degree. After all, the movie’s spiritual milieu is highly pre-Vatican II Catholic, in which suicides are condemned to hell, holy water acts like acid when splashed on a demon, angels have wings and there’s no room for any other

“God’s a kid with an ant farm, lady. He’s not planning anything.”

religious faith. But while Constantine works around the rules with the microscopic eye for loopholes of a kid calculating what sins to admit to in the confessional booth, he does not mistake them for any grander purpose.

Constantine’s appreciation of a random and ultimately uncaring order to things seems cold at first. When Angela says she doesn’t believe in the devil, he laconically replies, “You should, because he believes in you." His attitude is understandable, given that he has advanced lung cancer and already knows he's condemned to hell because of an earlier suicide attempt.

However, Constantine's mindset could actually be seen as more of a Buddhist perspective on the frequently unbelievable and horrifying things he witnesses. His take brings to mind the dictum posited by ninth century Buddhist monk Lin Chi, who told his followers that if they met the Buddha on the road, they should kill him, in order to truly free themselves from potentially imprisoning cant and ideology.

Similarly, Constantine has given up wondering what the purpose behind everything is. Given the horrors he's witnessed ("take it from me, two minutes in hell is a lifetime"), embracing randomness is a survival technique. And considering the inability of most people to have any say in their ultimate destiny, a cruel world can seem far less cruel if one doesn't believe there is any overarching plan for those inside it. Rather than devoting your life to exploring the problem of evil or banging your head against the question of why bad things seem to plague good people, you'd be wise to embrace Ecclesiastes and Occam in equal measure: Shit happens. You can't control what happens to you, so stop trying. Instead, embrace the only thing you can control—your attitude.

Sometimes, arbitrariness can be bliss.

STEEL CITY
CORP.

—*The Book of* The Lake House,
Chapter 8, Verse 10

KEANECDOTES

Minor Miracles from the Patron Saint of Whoa

Pursue Your Passions, and Friendships Will Follow

There is a lot to be said about the comforts of home, no matter who you are. For a Canadian, that means the bone-crunching speed of a hockey game, even in a parking lot.

THE INTERNET and this book are full of examples of Keanu being a good sport, but even his most dedicated fans might not know he's also good at sports, finding comfort as many do in letting his competitive nature run wild for a few minutes. In an infamous Reddit AMA, Keanu revealed that when he first arrived in Los Angeles as a 20-year-old aspiring actor, he happened to run into some guys at a gas station carrying hockey gear. Feeling out of place in his new Hollywood surroundings, he asked if he could join their game. Keanu, the former goalie for his high school team, ended up playing in their regular pickup game for the next decade, finding a little of his own unique Canadian zen in the middle of LA. So put yourself out there. You could end up forging friendships that transcend fame and fortune.

"Grief changes shape, but it never ends."

—Keanu Reeves

KEANECDOTES

Minor Miracles from the Patron Saint of Whoa

Freely Offer Kindness*

Keanu doesn't judge by what people drive—he just wants to make sure everyone gets where they're going.

IN 2020, IF PEOPLE saw Octavia Spencer broken down by the side of the road, most of them would jump at the chance to help the Oscar-nominated actress. But when she was still an up-and-comer and broke down on her way to an audition, car after car passed the sweatpants-clad Spencer's bird-poop-covered beater. Until Keanu Reeves happened by.

According to Spencer's retelling of the incident, Keanu arrived on his motorcycle and immediately offered to help. Starstruck and embarrassed by the state of her car, Spencer asked Keanu if he could sit in the front seat and steer while she pushed the car off the road. Keanu insisted they do it the other way 'round and soon had Spencer safely on her way. The lesson: No matter who you are, you can always find a moment to pay someone else a kindness—you never know who they're going to be.

* (And Muscle)

If you're going to kill someone's dog, check their resume first.

—*The Book of* John Wick, *Chapter 4, Verse 28*

Shoot the Hostage

Like Keanu in Speed, when life puts you in an untenable situation, take a breath and remove its leverage.

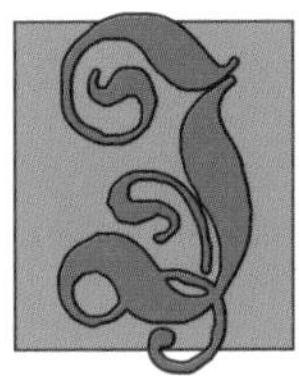

N THE 1994 thriller *Speed*, Keanu Reeves plays Jack Traven, a Los Angeles Police Department S.W.A.T. officer tasked with stopping psychopathic bomber Howard Payne (Dennis Hopper) from detonating a city bus. There is (as you know) one catch: If the bus travels below 50 miles per hour, it will explode. He demands $3.7 million for his diabolic handiwork before taunting Jack, asking, "What do you do?"

"What do you do?" is of course a callback to an earlier moment of tension between Jack and Payne, whose plan to keep an entire elevator full of civilians from punching the clock was foiled by the upstart

Keanu enduring the most stressful rush hour of all time.

S.W.A.T. star and his partner Harry (Jeff Daniels). Before Payne takes Harry hostage, Harry famously asks: "All right, pop quiz. Airport, gunman with one hostage. He's using her for cover; he's almost to a plane. You're a hundred feet away... Jack?" Jack's response is both a lesson in game theory and a strategy for success: Shoot the hostage.

Not in the face. Do it like Jack does Harry—right in the leg. By removing his partner from the equation, Jack takes away Payne's ability to move quickly with cover, as well as his leverage in the negotiation.

"When someone says they'll kill you if you don't play the game their way, what else have you got to lose?"

"Let me walk away or I'll kill your buddy" is a false binary—you always have other options, such as firing on your buddy yourself.

Keanu's Jack continues to out-maneuver his opponent in this way throughout the film. Whether it's by choosing to get on the bus himself once it's reached 50mph and armed with the bomb, sliding underneath the bus on a miniscule wheeled platform while it races down the highway to try and disarm the bomb, directing the bus to an airport so it can drive around safely in circles without the prying eyes of the press signaling the bus's every move to the bomber, or using the bus's closed-circuit camera system against the bomber in order to covertly sneak everyone to safety, pushing his "shoot the hostage" mentality to its most logical conclusion. After all, it's hard to blow up a bus full of hostages if none of them are on it.

Time and again, Jack refuses to play by the bomber's rules—even when he knows breaking them could have disastrous consequences (RIP Helen). When someone says they'll kill you if you don't play the game their way, what else have you got to lose? Why play by the rules when they're already cheating?

So what do you do? This pop quiz's answer isn't solely applicable for LAPD hotshots. If you're in a situation where you're being forced to choose between a set of terrible circumstances, turn the tables by pulling the trigger on an off-the-table choice that equally cripples your opponent. A boozed-up buddy refusing to hand over his keys? Slash his tires. Boss says no on a raise request? Politely explain you're quitting without notice. When you take away the idea of leverage, you even the playing field and can sometimes turn the tables on your opponent.

Just don't actually shoot anyone. This lesson is purely metaphorical.

Sometimes simple things are the most difficult things to achieve.

—Keanu Reeves

Minor Miracles from the Patron Saint of Whoa

Patience Is a Virtue, No Matter Your Station

When Keanu doesn't get the VIP treatment, he doesn't demand his privilege—he understands time spent waiting is still time spent being alive.

WHEN WE THINK of movie stars, one of the last things we tend to picture them doing is waiting in line—for anything. From the Staples Center to Splash Mountain, the A-listers wait for nothing and no one. Not so for Keanu, who represents the opposite of the "Don't you know who I am?" celebrity stereotype. After arriving at the wrap party for his 2016 film *Exposed*, Keanu found himself unrecognized by the doormen and relegated to the back of the line. But rather than use his clout to get in while the other cast and crew stood patiently in the New York rain, Keanu took his place and waited along with them, ultimately showing up 20 minutes late to his own celebration. It just goes to show that the party will always wait for you when you are the party.

In the future, humanity's hope will rest with a dolphin. Be prepared.

—*The Book of* Johnny Mnemonic, *Chapter 10, Verse 10*

The man who embraces his mediocre nothingness shines greater than any.

—Keanu Reeves,
Always Be My Maybe (2019)

Robert M Pirsig
ZEN and the ART of
MOTORCYCLE
Maintenance
MUJI for the
JOHN
WICK

Minor Miracles from the Patron Saint of Whoa

Stand for Something

Commuters in every major city got some required viewing when Keanu reminded them how to be a better passenger—and human.

"BE EXCELLENT to each other" is a phrase made famous by Keanu early in his career, but decades later it's still one credo he holds dear. In 2011, the A-lister proved it by doing something most commuting New Yorkers can't be bothered with even if a pregnant woman's water breaks directly in front of them on the Q train. Keanu, on the other hand, offered his seat to a stranger without so much as a second thought. It's a sad commentary on the world we live in that such a simple act of kindness is newsworthy, but the silver lining is that there are plenty of people out there like Keanu, ready to step in when it counts. And thankfully for the rest of us, someone on the subway was able to film the event, uploading it to YouTube and putting a few of Keanu's good vibes out there for all of us to learn from. Let your actions be excellent—the life you change could be your own.

If you're going to make a deal with the devil, you better be a damned good lawyer.

—*The Book of* The Devil's Advocate, *Chapter 18, Verse 6*

Don't Lose Your Shadow

Always keep an eye on your dark side. As A Scanner Darkly suggests, you never know when it will turn on you.

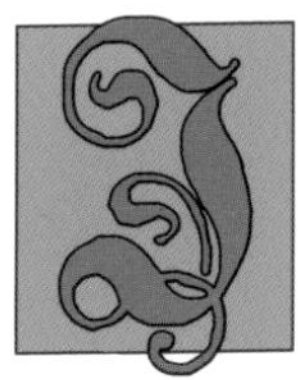

N RICHARD LINKLATER's fuzzily dystopic, animated nightmare *A Scanner Darkly* (2006), Keanu plays Bob Arctor, a guy who is living more than one life and realizes too late the danger of ignoring his other self. On the surface, Bob is just another junkie strung out on the brain-scrambling "Substance D" that has turned much of law enforcement into one massive surveillance apparatus. But even as Bob and his motor-mouthed drug-fiend roomies (Woody Harrelson, Robert Downey, Jr.) are spinning paranoid spiels, it turns out they actually are being watched—by Bob himself.

A phantasmagorical riff on Philip K. Dick's novel about the years and friends he lost to addiction, *A Scanner Darkly* wears its science fiction lightly.

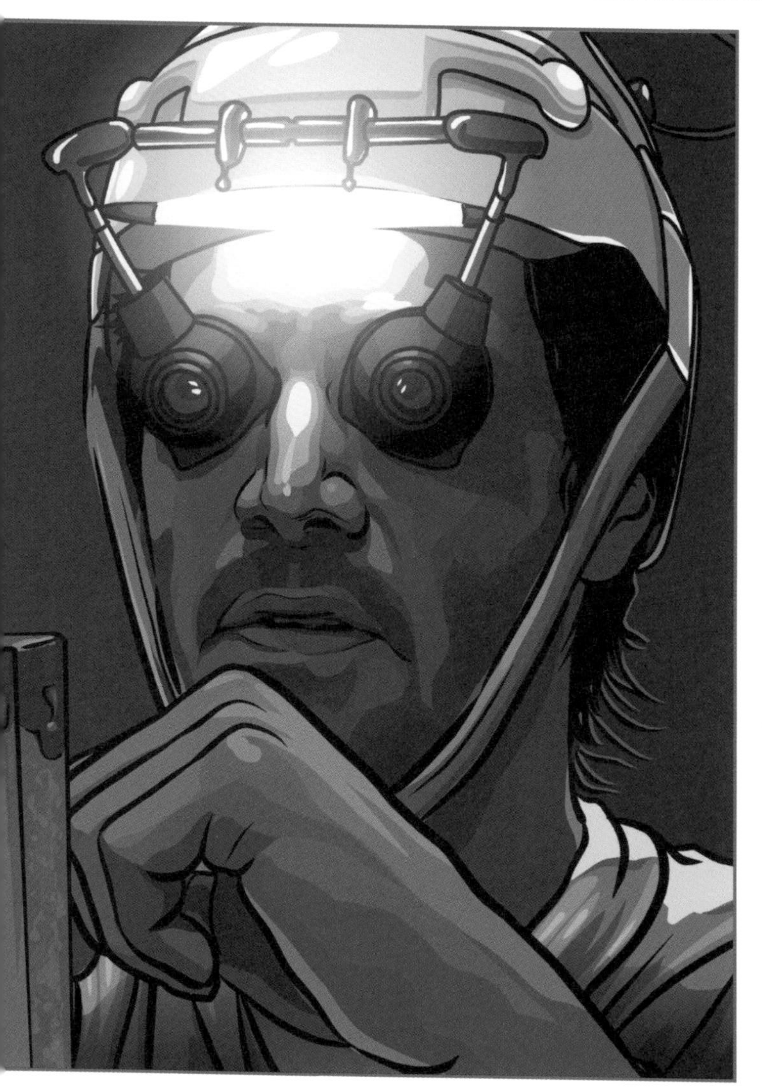

Keanu as Bob (or is it Fred?) in *A Scanner Darkly*.

Set just "seven years from now," the surveillance technology isn't terribly advanced, with one exception. When Bob puts on the identity-blurring "scramble suit" to stay anonymous at the police station, he is referred to as "Fred" while watching footage of himself. "I know Bob Arctor," Bob says at one point about himself. "He's a good person."

Whether it's Substance D's fraying of his neural pathways or an attempt to remove himself from culpability and guilt, Bob has mentally split himself into two men: "Bob" and "Fred." The Fred side of

"Only the fool can permanently disregard the conditions of his own nature."

his personality is aware of Bob but not vice versa. While this would make for a fantastic, if somewhat dark, sitcom premise, it doesn't bode well for Bob's sanity—no matter how much he keeps it together on the surface. In one scene, a seemingly calm, cool and collected Bob lays down some classically Keanu Zen wisdom, assuring a bugging-out friend that "the most dangerous kind of person is the one who's afraid of his own shadow." But this statement runs contrary to one of the film's central lessons—the reality is, our shadows might be the things we should fear most.

Carl Jung, who knew a few things about the subconscious goings-on Bob is tangling with, posited that every person has a shadow self of submerged impulses. This shadow could become potentially darker and more sinister the more it is ignored by the conscious self. "Only the fool can permanently disregard the conditions of his own nature," Jung wrote in *Civilization in Transition*. Not acknowledging the reality of your shadow self is a recipe for disaster. (It is also in part what Keanu was talking about in *Shadows*, his 2016 poetry/photography collaboration with Alexandra Grant: "Me and my shadow / and it still doesn't help.")

"What does the scanner see?" Bob wonders later about just what Fred is actually witnessing. "Does it see into me? Into us?" This is often read as an ominous suggestion, and for good reason in these times of omniscient surveillance. But Bob has a different take: "I hope it sees clearly because I can't any longer see into myself. I see only murk."

By refusing to give credence to the other side of his personality, Bob has blinded himself to it; there is no way to see a shadow in the dark. Bob, therefore, gave his friend incomplete advice. It's one thing not to be afraid of your shadow—it's another to ignore it.

Keep an eye on your dark side, or you may wake one day to realize it's swallowed up all your light.

It is incredibly empowering to know that your future is in your hands.

—Keanu Reeves

STOOD
STILL
STOOD
STILL
EARTH
STOOD
STILL
EARTH
STOOD
STILL
EARTH
STOOD
STILL
All my best
20/3/14

KEANECDOTES

Minor Miracles from the Patron Saint of Whoa

Go the Extra Mile, Even if It's Awkward

When a flustered fan made a Keanu sighting a tad weird, the star was there to save the day.

AS THE THIRD installment of Keanu's *John Wick* trilogy hit theaters in 2019, a fan took to the internet to share a Keanu story that proves just how much he cares about the people who enjoy his films—even if doing so is hampered by traditional social structures. A Twitter user revealed that while filming the *Matrix* trilogy in Australia, Keanu had come into the theater where they were working to see a movie. Hoping to sneakily score an autograph on the necessary receipt, the fan offered Keanu their employee discount on the ticket, which Keanu would need to sign to accept. But the actor, true-to-form, declined because he wasn't actually an employee. A few minutes later, there was a knock at the box office's back door: Keanu had returned, a signed receipt for a concession stand ice cream in hand. Keanu explained he'd had an epiphany: the attendant probably wanted his autograph. Keanu then threw the ice cream away (!) suggesting he purchased the treat solely to sign the receipt for a teenage fan. Remember: It only takes a few seconds to make someone's day. Try.

The only thing more dangerous than a bored teenager is two bored teenagers.

—*The Book of* Knock Knock, *Chapter 17, Verse 2*

Always Give One More Chance

As we learn from The Day the Earth Stood Still, fatalism can run afoul of forgiveness. It's always better to choose the latter.

N THE ENTIRELY unnecessary yet somehow still enjoyable 2008 remake of *The Day the Earth Stood Still*, Keanu plays the alien Klaatu. He enters the story by descending from a shimmering orb that plants itself in the middle of Central Park, intent on delivering a history-reshaping message—a sort of inverse of the Circle K scene in *Bill & Ted's Excellent Adventure*. Klaatu is just about to let humanity know their destructive and short-sighted ways have been brought to the attention of various extraterrestrial civilizations—making them think it's time to reboot Earth without mankind. Then a soldier shoots him for no good reason.

This appears to prove Klaatu's point. Nevertheless, at the movie's crucial moment, he stalks into a

Keanu takes a stroll in *The Day the Earth Stood Still.*

blizzard of city-devouring nanotech insects (it's a long story) just to give humanity another chance at proving itself. This development presents a pivot for Keanu away from the surf-dude wisdom he dispensed in earlier movies and takes him one step past the action-flick Chosen One of *The Matrix*. It also shows him as a resigned-to-fate figure whose Morpheus-esque utterances appear cold-blooded when he first takes human form (asked "Are you human?" he replies, "My body is") before his later pivot to benevolent sacrifice.

Whether or not Earth would be better off without people is not a new question. The optimistic Gaia hypothesis from the early 1970s postulated that every living thing on the planet functions as one self-regulating organism that can counterbalance any damage humans might cause. On the other end of the spectrum is the Medea hypothesis, which argues in essence that organic life's hunger for carbon will ultimately annihilate the biosphere long before a cooling sun makes the planet uninhabitable.

"At the precipice, we change."

Klaatu seems more of a strict Medean. "I came to save the Earth," he tells the scientist Helen (Jennifer Connelly). "If you die," he says, "the Earth survives." Apparently, the known universe has more expendable sentient species than life-sustaining planets, so his dire equation has logic behind it. Her argument is not the stronger one. It boils down to: We'll do better, we promise. A better riposte to his saying "Your problem is not technology, the problem is you" might have been: "Hey, maybe you could have showed up a century ago and given us a deadline?"

Nevertheless, something in her appeal triggers Klaatu's latent generosity of spirit. He already signaled the potential for this in one scene where, to avoid arrest, Klaatu kills a police officer by hitting him with a car and then MacGyver's him back to life with a car battery and a fingerful of all-purpose alien healing goop. Klaatu is further pushed to reconsider his position by an even more earnest professor (John Cleese), who argues that it's only at the moment of true danger when new potential can arise: "At the precipice, we change." Deciding hope beats fatalism, Klaatu walks into that nanotech insect storm.

In an age of rising sea levels, global pandemics and widespread addiction, to say nothing of the unregulated ennui brought on by social media, it's tempting to think it's too late for any of us to change our circumstances or better ourselves. But it's important to remember you've only given up when you've given in. We must choose to both acknowledge and forgive our own faults if we have any hope of moving past the damage they've caused. Yes, things may not get better. But they certainly won't if we abandon all hope and metaphorically welcome the flesh-devouring nanobots with open arms. The only way to fight fatalism is with hope—even when facing the end of the world.

o matter how successful, kind or handsome you are, you're no match for Jack Nicholson.

—*The Book of* Something's Gotta Give, *Chapter 7, Verse 3*

LATE
SHOW

Minor Miracles from the Patron Saint of Whoa

Live Like You Want to be Missed

On *The Late Show* in 2019, Keanu gave an eloquent answer to one of the world's most difficult questions.

WHEN YOUR reputation is one of zen-like patience and understanding, it's inevitable that your interviewers will eventually ask you some deep philosophical questions. When you're also an A-list actor and the interviewer happens to be the host of *The Late Show*, those questions get even more extreme. But Keanu was more than game when Stephen Colbert asked him in May 2019 what he thinks happens when we die. Rather than deflect the question or offer one of the many clichés available to him, Keanu spoke from the heart. His answer encompassed everything from our inability to know the specifics of death while we're living to the inevitability of loss. The most impressive part? The answer came in the form of a short, single-clause sentence: "I know that the ones who love us will miss us." The lesson: We can't be certain of what comes next, but living with certainty is a surefire way to ensure we impact the lives we'll leave behind.

People can't be excellent to you unless you're being excellent to yourself.

—Keanu, *Keanu* (2016)

Don't Be Afraid of Asymmetry

The Matrix changed the way many of us view the world, and at its core is a battle cry to do the unexpected.

A GOOD PART OF THE Wachowskis' mind-bending cyberpunk action franchise *The Matrix* (1999) is taken up with people telling Keanu's hacker hero Neo what to do, how to do it and why things are the way they are. Throughout much of the first installment, he is schooled by the mysterious Morpheus (Laurence Fishburne) and Trinity (Carrie-Anne Moss) in how what he thinks of as reality is just a computer simulation (the Matrix) run by a malevolent AI that has enslaved humanity. Neo learns he's spent much of his life as a battery. He discovers the truth behind deja vus. Soon, he knows kung fu. But despite all that learning, Neo seems to do best when he ignores some of what he has been told.

Keanu prepares to move faster than a speeding bullet.

A classic "Chosen One" protagonist of the kind that has proliferated in the post-*Star Wars* era, Neo would appear to have all his actions laid out for him by the prophecies of his coming. At first, he goes along with the program, gamely dropping down the rabbit hole once he has taken the red pill revealing the horror of humanity's reality, proving highly adept in the programs that train his avatar how to bend the programmed rules of the Matrix to his advantage (particularly in flouting the law of gravity).

"'No one's ever done anything like this.' Neo replies, "That's why it's going to work.'"

But although Neo takes to subverting the Matrix with impressive speed, it's only when Morpheus is captured by the sadistic sentient programs known as Agents that Neo truly proves he is The One. Neo proposes to rescue Morpheus from a facility crawling with Agents, a seemingly impossible task since Neo's confederates in the human resistance have told him the only way to survive meeting an Agent is to run. Trinity is resistant: "No one's ever done anything like this." Neo replies, "That's why it's going to work."

Any good tactician will tell you that the element of surprise is crucial to victory. Sun Tzu wrote that all warfare is based on deception. That does not always mean confusing the enemy about your angle of approach. Attacking in a way that has never been considered before not only provides the element of surprise but can sometimes mean no defense has been prepared. In the case of Neo, not only does he face down Agents instead of running from them, he showcases a hitherto unseen ability: dodging bullets by slowing down time and bending like a gymnast. All of this throws the Agents off their game; and that's before Neo realizes he can fly like Superman.

Whether a dentist dispensing pearls of wisdom (*Thumbsucker*), circus daredevil with an existential side (*Toy Story 4*) or metalhead who challenges Death to a game of Battleship (*Bill & Ted's Bogus Journey*), Keanu's characters often make a point of upending expectations. He manages to finally save the world at the end of the interminable *The Matrix Revolutions* by again doing what nobody ever thought possible: While the rest of humanity is hunkered down in their rave fort trying to stave off their inevitable annihilation by the machines, Neo is zooming into the heart of the AI, trying to make a deal.

Nobody ever thought of trying that before. Maybe you should, too. When facing your own "impossible" battles, trying the impossible might be the only thing that pays off.

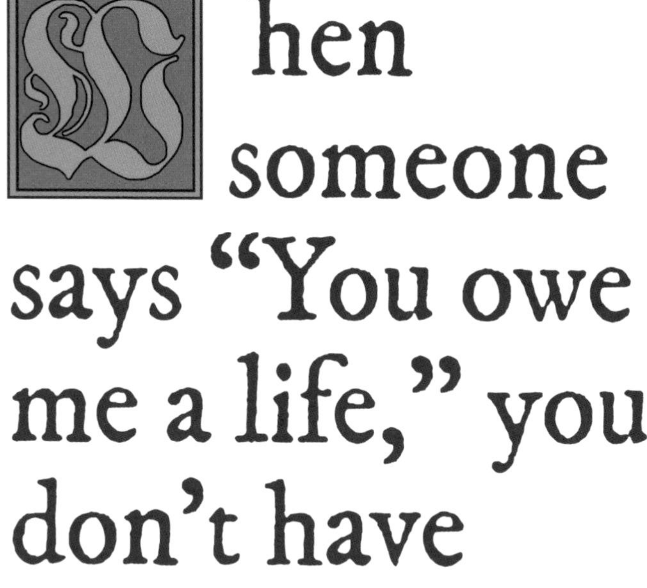

When someone says "You owe me a life," you don't have to take them literally.

—*The Book of* Man of Tai Chi, *Chapter 5, Verse 22*

ARCH
MOTORCYCLE
COMPANY

Minor Miracles from the Patron Saint of Whoa

Expand Your Horizons by Expanding Others'

A lifelong fan of motorcycle racing, Keanu has a fleet of bikes to play with—and he's sharing his passions with the next generation.

WHEN KEANU and his friend Gard Hollinger founded ARCH motorcycles, they were fulfilling their own childhood dreams of becoming not just motorcycle riders, but creators of new and exciting bikes. But true to the generous nature he's shown time and again, Keanu has found a way to turn his passion project into a way of helping others realize their own motorhead dreams. At just 13 years old, Damian Jigalov was already such a proven racing prodigy that he was fully primed to make his professional debut on the Italian circuit. Professional motorsport, however, is hardly a sustainable pursuit within the financial limits of one's teenage years. Enter: Keanu. After watching Jigalov compete in the Pre-Moto3 class in the Italian Speed Championship, Keanu and his partners sat down with the phenom to sponsor him through ARCH bikes. Now an ARCH rider, Jigalov is pursuing his dreams at the highest level thanks to Keanu's generosity. When you're lucky enough to achieve your own dreams, you should help others achieve theirs when you can.

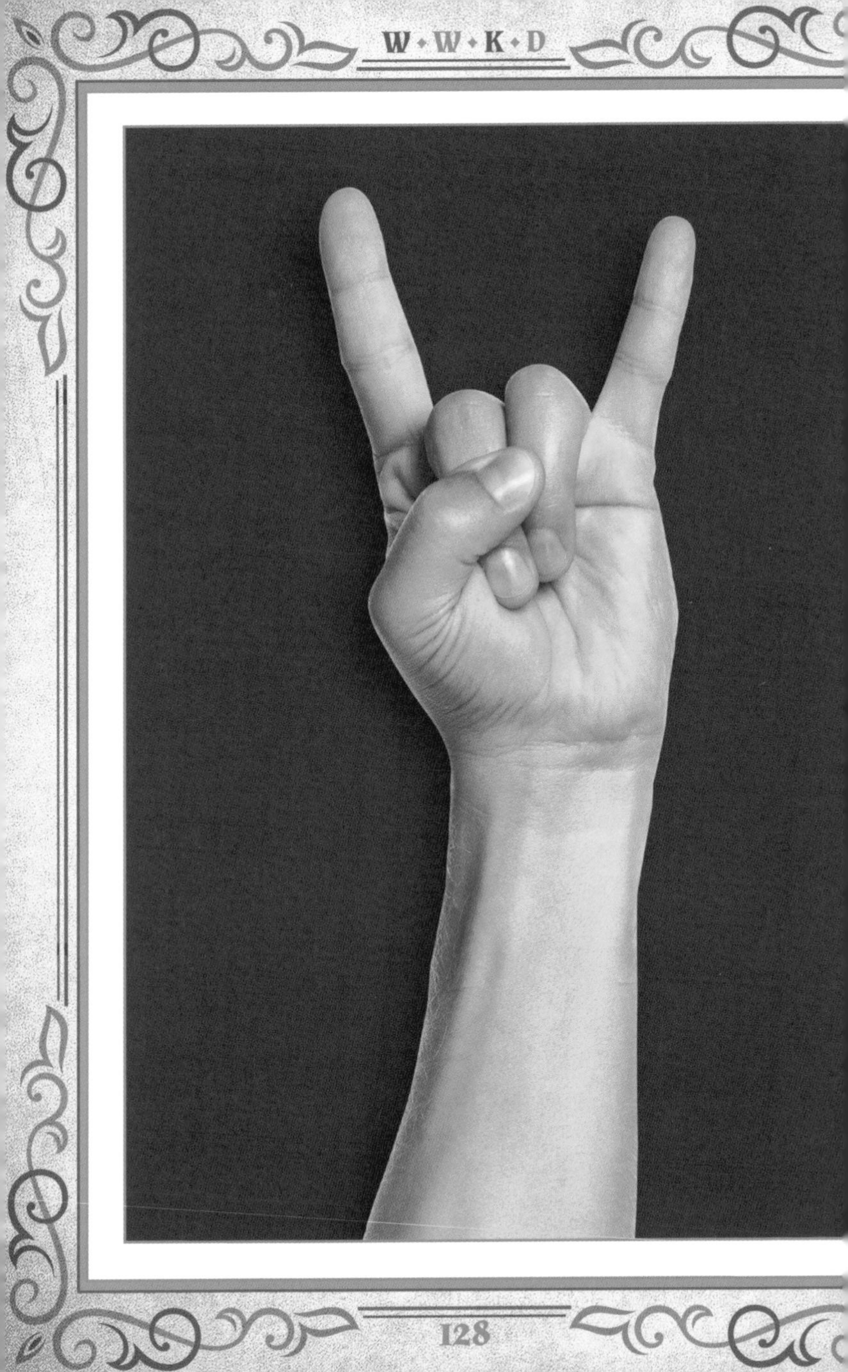

Be excellent to each other.... ...party on, dudes!

—The Wyld Stallyns,
Bill & Ted's Excellent Adventure (1989)

SENTINELS
16

KEANECDOTES

Minor Miracles from the Patron Saint of Whoa

Get the Job Done, No Matter What

Valuing quality over monetary reward is something few people learn to do. Even fewer are Keanu Reeves.

ONCE ONE HAS worked their way up the Hollywood totem pole to the A-list, "pay cut" tends to cease being a phrase in their vocabulary. The highest-paid stars can command percentages of a film's overall budget that seem, to the layman, to translate into impossible sums, and few who have tasted the fruits of such handsome fees are willing to give them up. This is not so for Keanu, who has proven several times throughout his career that creating the best possible film matters more to him than lining his own pockets. For instance, when pre-production for *The Devil's Advocate* (1997) seemed to be veering in a direction that didn't include Al Pacino, Keanu readily volunteered for a pay cut so the film's budget could accommodate the living legend. Similarly, when it looked like his 2000 football comedy *The Replacements* might have to go on without Gene Hackman in the cast, Keanu reportedly agreed to a cut of no less than 90 percent in his own salary to entice the Oscar-winner into joining the cast. His generosity with his salary doesn't only extend to fellow actors, either—he reportedly took a $75 million dollar cut from his proceeds from *The Matrix* films to share it with the crew. Sure, money comes and goes. But as Keanu knows, quality is something people will always remember.

ever
trust the
commercials.

—*The Book of* Toy Story 4,
Chapter 6, Verse 12

To Thine Own Self Be True

John Wick teaches us the importance of maintaining one's personal autonomy in spite of outside pressures. He also kills 77 people.

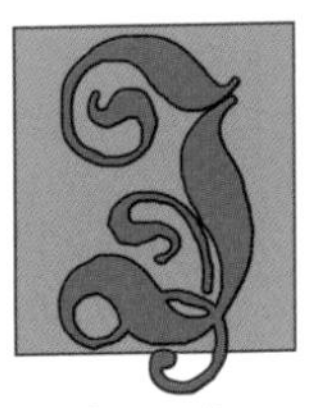

N THE PARADIGM-SHIFTING 2014 shoot-'em-up *John Wick*, Reeves stars as the titular grumpy and socially isolated former hitman, who left the killing-for-cash game after the crushing loss of his wife Helen. Consoled by Daisy, the beagle Helen left as a cuddly support system, the widowed Wick broods in his villain-minimalist home and tools around in a gloriously restored classic Ford Mustang.

But the Freemason-esque world of criminality undergirding this movie series does not let its citizens go without a fight. After an irritating Russian Mafioso starts messing with the violence-averse Wick, the conflict escalates fast. When the thugs kill Daisy, Wick's stoicism shatters like the

Keanu as the sixth-commandment flouting John Wick.

floor he sledgehammers through to pull out the death-dealing weapons of the trade he thought was behind him.

As John Locke argues in *An Essay Concerning Human Understanding* (1689), personal identity is a continuum of consciousness that changes over time but remains fundamentally the same, which means Wick will always be the guy who once killed three men with a pencil. Pacifist John Wick getting pummeled is ultimately the same John Wick who takes out an entire nightclub of gunmen without mussing his impeccable suit. His state is a question of conditions, not of being.

Later in his spiraling chain of vengeance, Wick says, “People keep asking if I’m back and I haven’t really had an answer. But now, yeah, I’m thinking I’m back.” This doesn’t just refer to all his old running buddies wondering if he’s back in the killing game—it’s a callback to the scene when a cop comes by his house to check on a disturbance and asks, “You working again?”

Wick’s dilemma is one faced by most cinematic heroes: How far can the world push you before you push back?

“When they ask him ‘Are you back?’ what they are really asking him is, ‘What kind of person are you?’”

Think of Patrick Swayze’s philosopher-king-bouncer in *Roadhouse*, pitying the mooks who mistake his quiet gravitas for an inability to deliver roundhouse kicks and rip throats. But for the average person who doesn’t live in a world like Wick’s (one seemingly conjured by John Woo set loose in a Dan Brown novel by way of Elmore Leonard), the decision he faces is still relatable: At what point do we let the world define us rather than defining ourselves in the world?

According to social identity theory, people are viewed relative to their place in society. This perception is influenced by the categorization factors (e.g., net worth, talents, class, race, gender) society uses to determine a person's value. Wick's specific place in the movie's baroquely rule-bound criminal society, alongside his ability to provide a sought-after service with crisp professionalism, once provided him with a high value. After Wick abandoned that place and resulting value, however, its members have no way of dealing with or even understanding him. When they ask him, "Are you back?" what they are really asking him is, "What kind of person are you?" Much like all of us when beholding the quiet determination of Keanu, they become flustered.

Ideally, we would all exist as fully free individuals judged by our actions and the content of our souls. But in addition to being wise and a smart dresser, Wick is a realist. By initially striving to eschew vengeance, he has shown an appreciation for patience. But he also understands for the world to comprehend what he wants (freedom, an unwrecked Mustang, a still-breathing wife, a not-dead dog), he must present himself in a way that can be understood.

Am I back? Yes, I am back, Wick says. He is working again. But rather than voicing that return as a tragic complaint, he frames it as an acknowledgment of his nature. Wick is not back so much as he is a man who understands he never truly went away.

Don't ask too many questions: just enjoy your steak.

—*The Book of* The Matrix,
Chapter 10, Verse 1

Keanu's Tacos
2-TACOS
FREE
of charge
DRINK
POISSONS

KEANECDOTES

Minor Miracles from the Patron Saint of Whoa

Give What You Can Whenever You Can

The star's generosity is so legendary, you'd be forgiven for assuming he saved Christmas. (Spoiler alert: he did.)

IT SHOULD BE CLEAR by now that Keanu respects and appreciates those who work on his films. Whether he's taking pay cuts to work with his idols or gifting motorcycles to his stuntmen, he's not shy about showing his love or sharing his largesse. When Keanu found out one of the set builders on the *Matrix* films was suffering through a particularly challenging financial time, he offered the builder a Christmas bonus (as he had done for many crew members). But inside this particular yuletide care package was a whopping $20,000—enough to ease the builder's struggles and give him the opportunity for a stress-free holiday. His giving isn't simply seasonal. Keanu even went so far as to buy breakfast and lunch for his crew nearly every day on the set of *Chain Reaction*, paying for food trucks to deliver quality eats from his favorite spots. While you might not have the resources to offer similar gifts on a regular basis, you should never underestimate how much of an impact a gesture of appreciation—big or small—can have on those you rely on. Pay things forward and dividends will follow.

Don't fool yourself into thinking you've got the answer.... The trick is living without an answer. I think.

—Dr. Perry Lyman, *Thumbsucker* (2005)

Media Lab Books
For inquiries, call 646-838-6637

Published by Topix Media Lab
14 Wall Street, Suite 4B
New York, NY 10005

Printed in Korea

ISBN-13: 978-1-948174-65-7
ISBN-10: 1-948174-65-0

Cover: Christopher Jue/Getty Images. Digital Imaging by Eric Heintz

7 AF Archive/Alamy; 10 United Archives GmbH/Alamy; 17 Moviestore Collection Ltd/Alamy; 20 AF Archive/Alamy; 27 AF Archive/Alamy; 30 Entertainment Pictures/Alamy; 34 Allstar Picture Library/Alamy; 41 Warner Bros/Everett Collection; 44 United Archives GmbH/Alamy; 51 Collection Christophel/Alamy; 54 Photo 12/Alamy; 61 Collection Christophel/Alamy; 64 Collection Christophel/ Alamy; 71 TCD/Prod.DB/Alamy; 74 AF Archive/Alamy; 82 TCD/Prod.DB/Alamy; 85 Photo 12/Alamy; 92 TCD/Prod.DB/Alamy; 98 Collection Christophel/Alamy; 101 PictureLux/The Hollywood Archive/ Alamy; 108 TCD/Prod.DB/Alamy; 111 Allstar Picture Library/Alamy; 114 TCD/Prod.DB/Alamy; 118 Warner Bros/Everett Collection; 121 PictureLux/The Hollywood Archive/Alamy; 124 Allstar Picture Library/Alamy; 132 PictureLux/The Hollywood Archive/Alamy; 135 Allstar Picture Library/Alamy; 138 TCD/Prod.DB/Alamy; All additional photography: Shutterstock

All illustrations by Jan Feindt

PA-F20-1

Acknowledgements

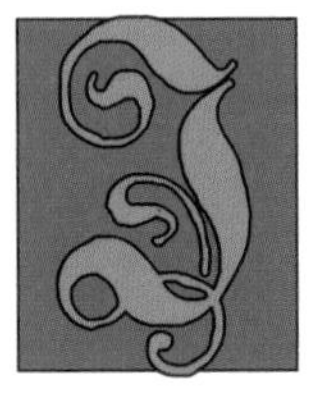

T TAKES A VILLAGE to make a book and this one is no different. I consider myself very lucky to have been asked to contribute to this project and am deeply thankful for the ingenuity, artistry—particularly by illustrator Jan Feidt—and dedication put into it by Jeff Ashworth, Courtney Kerrigan, Phil Sexton, Juliana Sharaf and the rest of the team at Media Lab Books. They created this rabbit hole and were kind enough to let me follow them down it.

CHRIS BARSANTI is a member of the Online Film Critics Society and the author of several books, including *Filmology* and *The Sci-Fi Movie Guide*. His writing has appeared in *Film Journal International*, *PopMatters*, the *Minneapolis Star-Tribune*, *Film Threat*, *The Barnes & Noble Review*, *Publishers Weekly* and the *Chicago Tribune*. He has never seen *Forrest Gump* and, at this point, most likely never will.